16 KNITTED SHOE STYLES FOR BABY'S FIRST YEAR

CLASSIC KICKS
FOR LITTLE FEET

Helga Spitz

Edition Michael Fischer GmbH, 2017
www.emf-verlag.de

This translation of BABYSHÜHCHEN TICK - STRICKEN, first
published in Germany by Edition Michael Fischer GmbH in 2017,
is published by arrangement with Silke Bruenink Agency,
Munich, Germany.

CLASSIC KICKS
FOR LITTLE FEET

16 KNITTED SHOE STYLES
FOR BABY'S FIRST YEAR

Helga Spitz

Table of Contents

Eye-Catchers

Summer, Sun, Sandals

Knitting Instructions

The Basics

Yarn Substitutes

To help with finding yarns appropriate for the projects, we have provided a substitution chart with yarns readily available in the United States. Each project lists these substitute yarns in the materials list.

ORIGINAL YARN	YARN WEIGHTS	SUBSTITUTE YARN
Lang Yarns Merino 120 (merino superwash) 131yd/120m per 1¾oz/50g	(3)	Cascade Yarns 220 Superwash (superwash wool) 220yd/200m per 3½oz/100g
Lang Yarns Merino 150 (merino superwash) 164yd/150m per 1¾oz/50g	(2)	DMC Woolly (merino wool) 135yd/124m per 1¾oz/50g
Lang Yarns Merino+ (merino superwash) 98yd/90m per 1¾ozoz/50g	(4)	Cascade Yarns 220 Superwash Aran (superwash merino wool) 150yd/137.5m per 3½oz/100g
Lang Yarns Classico (wool, nylon, cotton) 120yd/110m per1¾oz/50g	(4)	Cascade Yarns 220 Superwash (superwash wool) 220yd/200m per 3½oz/100g
Online Linie 164 Java (cotton, viscose) 173yd/158m per 1¾oz/50g	(3)	Cascade Yarns Sunseeker (cotton/acrylic) 246yd/200m per 3½oz/100g
Online Linie 99 Babysoft (acrylic) 202yd/185m per 1¾oz/50g	(3)	Cascade Yarns North Shore (acrylic) 220yd/200m per 3½oz/100g

Sizes

This book offers three sizes of shoes. The approximate length of the bottom of the sole for each size is as follows:

0–3 months: 3½"/9cm
3–6 months: 4"/10cm
6–9 months: 4½"/11.5cm

Each shoe style is given in only one size. If you would like to make a larger size, try working the pattern with a larger needle size and/or a heavier weight yarn. If you would like to make a smaller size, try working the pattern with a smaller needle size and/or a lighter weight yarn.

Standard Yarn Weight System

Categories of yarn, gauge ranges, and recommended needle and hook sizes

Yarn Weight Symbol & Category	**0** Lace	**1** Super Fine	**2** Fine	**3** Light	**4** Medium	**5** Bulky	**6** Super Bulky	**7** Jumbo
Type of Yarns in Category	Fingering 10-count crochet thread	Sock, Fingering, Baby	Sport, Baby	DK, Light Worsted	Worsted, Afghan, Aran	Chunky, Craft, Rug	Super Bulky, Roving	Jumbo, Roving
Knit Gauge Range* in Stockinette Stitch to 4 inches	33–40** sts	27–32 sts	23–26 sts	21–24 sts	16–20 sts	12–15 sts	7–11 sts	6 sts and fewer
Recommended Needle in Metric Size Range	1.5–2.25 mm	2.25—3.25 mm	3.25—3.75 mm	3.75—4.5 mm	4.5—5.5 mm	5.5—8 mm	8—12.75 mm	12.75 mm and larger
Recommended Needle U.S. Size Range	000–1	1 to 3	3 to 5	5 to 7	7 to 9	9 to 11	11 to 17	17 and larger
Crochet Gauge* Ranges in Single Crochet to 4 inch	32–42 double crochets**	21–32 sts	16–20 sts	12–17 sts	11–14 sts	8–11 sts	6–9 sts	5 sts and fewer
Recommended Hook in Metric Size Range	Steel*** 1.6–1.4 mm	2.25—3.5 mm	3.5—4.5 mm	4.5—5.5 mm	5.5—6.5 mm	6.5—9 mm	9—16 mm	16 mm and larger
Recommended Hook U.S. Size Range	Steel*** 6, 7, 8 Regular hook D 1	B–1 to E–4	E–4 to 7	7 to I–9	I–9 to K–10 1/2	K–10 1/2 to M–13	M–13 to Q	Q and larger

* GUIDELINES ONLY: The above reflect the most commonly used gauges and needle or hook sizes for specific yarn categories.

** Lace weight yarns are usually knitted or crocheted on larger needles and hooks to create lacy, openwork patterns. Accordingly, a gauge range is difficult to determine. Always follow the gauge stated in your pattern.

*** Steel crochet hooks are sized differently from regular hooks—the higher the number, the smaller the hook, which is the reverse of regular hook sizing

This Standards & Guidelines booklet and downloadable symbol artwork are available at: **YarnStandards.com**

For Tiny Dancers

Whether adorned with straps, bows, or buckles,
slippers are a must for little feet that itch to dance.

Slippers with Bows

Chunky bow ties make these casual slippers perfect
for a little dance around the house.

MATERIALS
1 3½oz/100g ball (220yd/200m)
of Cascade 220 Superwash
(superwash wool) in red
1 1¾oz/50g ball (135yd/124m) of
DMC Woolly (merino wool) in brown
1 set (5) size 4 (3.5mm) dpn
1 pair size 3 (3.25mm) needles
Stitch marker
Yarn needle
Optional: Elastic thread

GAUGE
25 sts and 52 rows to 4"/10cm over
garter st using larger needles and Woolly.
TAKE TIME TO CHECK GAUGE.

NOTE
If desired, work bind-off of top of shoe
holding yarn with elastic thread to help
pull in top edge.

SOLE
With larger needles and brown, cast on
32 sts. Divide sts evenly over 4 needles
(8 sts per needle). Join, taking care not
to twist sts, and place marker for beg of
rnd (back of shoe).
Work in garter st in rnds (purl 1 rnd,
knit 1 rnd) as follows:
Rnd 1 Purl.
Rnd 2 Needle 1: K1, M1, knit to end;

Needle 2: Knit to last st, M1, k1;
Needle 3: K1, M1, work to end;
Needle 4: Knit to last st, M1, k1—1 st
inc'd on each needle; 4 sts inc'd in total.
Repeat last 2 rnds 4 times more—13 sts
per needle; 52 sts in total.
Purl 3 rnds. Cut brown

SHOE
Join red. Knit 1 rnd.
Next rnd P13, [k1, p4] 5 times, k1, p13.

SHAPE TOE
Rnd 1 P13, [k1 in rnd below, p1, p2tog,
p1] 5 times, k1 in rnd below, p13—47 sts.
Rnd 2 P13, [k1, p3] 5 times, k1, p13.
Rnd 3 P13, [k1 in rnd below, p3] 5
times, k1 in rnd below, p13.
Rnd 4 P13, [k1, p1, p2tog] 5 times, k1,
p13—42 sts.
Rnd 5 P13, [k1 in rnd below, p2] 5
times, k1 in rnd below, p13.
Rnd 6 P13, [k1, p2] 5 times, k1, p13.
Rnd 7 P13, [k1 in rnd below, p2] 5
times, k1 in rnd below, p13.
Rnd 8 P13, [k1, p2] 5 times, k1, p13.
Rnd 9 P13, [k1 in rnd below, p2] 5
times, k1 in row below, p13.
Rnd 10 P13, [k1, p2tog] 5 times, k1,
p13—37 sts.
Bind off all sts knitwise.

FINISHING
Sew sole seam.

BOW
With smaller needles and red, cast on
34 sts. Bind off. Attach center to front
of slipper and tie in a bow.

Repeat from beginning for second shoe. ●

SIZE
0-3 MONTHS

Budding ballerinas will swoon for their first pair
of real ballet slippers, made just for them.

MATERIALS

1 1¾oz/50g ball (135yd/124m)
of DMC Woolly (merino wool)
each in white, burgundy, and brown
1 set (5) size 3 (3.25mm) dpn
Crochet hook size D-3 (3.25mm)
Stitch marker
Yarn needle
8 burgundy beads, 4mm
Optional: Elastic thread

GAUGE

26 sts and 52 rows to 4"/10cm over
garter st using size 3 (3.25mm) needles.
TAKE TIME TO CHECK GAUGE.

NOTE

If desired, work bind-off of top of shoe
holding yarn with elastic thread to help
pull in top edge.

SOLE

With white, cast on 32 sts. Divide sts
evenly over 4 needles (8 sts per needle).
Join, taking care not to twist sts, and
place marker for beg of rnd (back of
shoe).
Work in garter st in rnds (purl 1 rnd,
knit 1 rnd) as follows:
Rnd 1 Purl.
Rnd 2 Needle 1: K1, M1, knit to end;
Needle 2: Knit to last st, M1, k1;
Needle 3: K1, M1, knit to end;
Needle 4: Knit to last st, M1, k1—1 st
inc'd on each needle; 4 sts inc'd in total.
Repeat last 2 rnds 3 times more—12 sts
per needle; 48 sts in total.
Purl 2 rounds. Cut white.

SHOE

Join burgundy. Knit 2 rnds.

BEGIN SHORT ROWS

Rnd 1 K30, turn, work double st (see
page 62);
P11, turn, work double st;
K9, turn, work double st;
P7, turn, work double st;
Knit to end of round, working double sts
tog with corresponding sts on needle.
Rnd 2 Knit, working rem double sts tog
with corresponding sts on needle.
Rnd 3 K20, [k2tog] 4 times, k20—44 sts.
Rnd 4 Knit.
Rnd 5 K17, [k2tog, k2] twice, k2tog,
k17—41 sts.
Rnd 6 K20, k2tog, k19—40 sts.
Bind off as follows.
*K2tog, return st to LH needle; rep
from * until all sts are bound off.

FINISHING

Sew sole seam.

HEEL

With brown, cast on 16 sts. Divide sts
evenly over 4 needles (4 sts per needle).
Join, taking care not to twist sts, and
place marker for beg of rnd.
Work in garter st in rnds as follows:
Rnd 1 Purl.
Rnd 2 Needle 1: K1, M1, knit to end;
Needle 2: Knit to last st, M1, k1;
Needle 3: K1, M1, knit to end;
Needle 4: Knit to last st, M1, k1—1 st
inc'd on each needle; 4 sts inc'd in total.
Repeat last 2 rnds once more—6 sts per
needle; 24 sts in total. Bind off.
Sew center seam. Sew heel to back of
sole.

TIES

With crochet hook and burgundy, chain
80. Work slip st in each chain. Fasten off.
Repeat for second tie.
With ties held tog, sew ties to center
front of slipper and then tie in a bow.
Attach a bead to each end of both ties.

Weave in ends.

Repeat from beginning for second shoe.

SIZE
0-3 MONTHS

Mary Janes

For girls on the go, a buckle and strap make sure
these slippers can keep up with every step.

MATERIALS

1 1¾oz/50g ball (135yd/124m)
of DMC Woolly (merino wool)
each in teal and brown
1 set (5) size 3 (3.25mm) dpn
Stitch marker
Yarn needle
2 small silver buckles

GAUGE

26 sts and 52 rows to 4"/10cm over
garter st using size 3 (3.25mm) needles.
TAKE TIME TO CHECK GAUGE.

SOLE

Cut a 24"/61cm length of brown yarn
and place to side for later use as an extra
strand.

With brown, cast on 32 sts. Divide sts
evenly over 4 needles (8 sts per needle).
Join, taking care not to twist sts, and
place marker for beg of rnd (back of
shoe).

Work in garter st in rnds (purl 1 rnd,
knit 1 rnd) as follows:

Rnd 1 Purl.

Rnd 2 Needle 1: K1, M1, knit to end;
Needle 2: Knit to last st, M1, k1;
Needle 3: K1, M1, knit to end;

Needle 4: Knit to last st, M1, k1—1 st
inc'd on each needle; 4 sts inc'd in total.
Repeat last 2 rnds 5 times more, working
the last rnd with 2 strands of yarn held
tog—14 sts per needle; 56 sts in total.
Drop extra strand and knit 1 rnd.
Cut brown.

SHOE

Join teal. Knit 1 round.

SHAPE TOP

Rnd 1 K25, [M1, k2] 3 times, M1,
k25—60 sts.

Rnds 2–5 Knit.

Rnd 6 K25, [k2tog, k2] twice, k2tog,
k25—57 sts.

Rnd 7 K20, [k2tog, k2] 4 times, k2tog,
k19—52 sts.

BEGIN SHORT ROWS

Rnd 1 K38, turn, work double st (see
page 62);
P23, turn, work double st;
K3, [k2tog, k1] 5 times, k3, turn, work
double st;
P13, turn, work double st;
K3, [k2tog] twice, k3, turn, work double st;
P6, turn, work double st;
Knit to end of round, working double sts
tog with corresponding sts on needle.
Knit 1 rnd over all sts, working rem
double sts tog with corresponding sts on
needle. Bind off all sts.

FINISHING

Sew sole seam.

STRAP

With teal, cast on 5 sts. Work I-cord as
follows:

Row 1 K5, do not turn. Slide sts to right
tip of needle, pulling yarn across back of
work to work next row from RS.
Repeat row 1 for 3¼"/8cm. Bind off.
Sew straps to shoe, attaching buckle on
one end before sewing.

Weave in ends.

Repeat from beginning for second shoe. ●

Ankle Strap Slippers

Inspired by the ribbons on point shoes,
these lovelies will make twirling that much easier.

MATERIALS
1 1¾oz/50g ball (135yd/124m)
of DMC Woolly (merino wool)
each in pink and brown
1 set (5) each size 3 and 4
(3.25 and 3.5mm) dpn
Stitch marker
Yarn needle

GAUGE
25 sts and 52 rows to 4"/10cm over
garter st using larger needles.
TAKE TIME TO CHECK GAUGE.

SOLE
Cut a 24"/61cm length of brown yarn
and place to side for later use as an extra
strand.
With larger needles and brown, cast on
32 sts. Divide sts evenly over 4 needles
(8 sts per needle). Join, taking care not
to twist sts, and place marker for beg of
rnd (back of shoe).
Work in garter st in rnds (purl 1 rnd,
knit 1 rnd) as follows:
Rnd 1 Purl.
Rnd 2 Needle 1: K1, M1, knit to end;
Needle 2: Knit to last st, M1, k1;
Needle 3: K1, M1, knit to end;
Needle 4: Knit to last st, M1, k1—1 st
inc'd on each needle; 4 sts inc'd in total.
Repeat last 2 rnds 5 times more, working the last rnd with 2 strands of yarn
held tog—14 sts per needle; 56 sts in total. Drop extra strand and purl 2 rnds.
Cut brown.

SHOE
Join pink. Knit 1 rnd.

SHAPE TOP
Rnd 1 K23, [M1, k2] 5 times, M1, k23—
62 sts.
Rnds 2–5 Knit.
Rnd 6 K15, [k2tog, k4] 5 times, k2tog,
k15—56 sts.
Rnd 7 Knit.
Rnd 8 K15, [k2tog, k4] 4 times, k2tog,
k15—51 sts.
Rnd 9 Knit.
Rnd 10 K15, [k2tog] 5 times, k1, [k2tog]
5 times, k15—41 sts.
Rnd 11 Purl.
Rnd 12 Knit.
Bind off as follows:
*K2tog, return st to LH needle; rep
from * until all sts are bound off.

FINISHING
Sew sole seam.

STRAP
With smaller needles and pink, cast on 6
sts. Work I-cord as follows:
Rnd 1 K6, do not turn. Slide sts to right
tip of needle, pulling yarn across back of
work to work next row from RS.
Repeat rnd 1 for 10"/25cm. Bind off all sts.

HEEL TAB
With smaller dpn and A, cast on 4 sts.
Work I-cord as for straps for 1½"/4cm.
Bind off all sts.

Fold heel tab in half and sew to center of
back heel. Sew one end of strap to top of
shoe, thread through heel tab, cross second
half under first half and sew second end to
opposite edge at top of shoe (see photo).

Weave in ends.

Repeat from beginning for second shoe.●

The Big Outdoors

Warm boots are a must-have when there's a chill in the air.
With these, there will be no need to stop exploring!

SIZE
3-6 MONTHS

Cozy Boots

Comfy and cute, shearling-look boots are on-trend
as soon as the first autumn leaf drops.

MATERIALS
1 3½oz/100g hank (150yd/137.5m)
of Cascade 220 Superwash Aran
(wool) each in beige and gray
1 set (5) size 7 (4.5mm) dpn
Stitch marker
Yarn needle

GAUGE
19 sts and 34 rows to 4"/10cm over seed
st using size 7 (4.5mm) needles.
TAKE TIME TO CHECK GAUGE.

SEED STITCH
Rnd 1 *K1, p1; rep from * around.
Rnd 2 *P1, k1; rep from * around.
Repeat rnds 1 and 2 for seed st.

SOLE
Cut a 36"/91.5cm length of gray yarn
and place to side for later use as an
extra strand.
With gray, cast on 28 sts. Divide sts
evenly over 4 needles (7 sts per needle).
Join, taking care not to twist sts, and
place marker for beg of rnd (back of
shoe).
Work in seed stitch for 2 rnds.
Continue in seed st, as follows:
Rnd 1 Needle 1: K1, M1, work to end;
Needle 2: Work to last st, M1, k1;

Needle 3: K1, M1, work to end;
Needle 4: Work to last st, M1, k1—1 st
inc'd on each needle; 4 sts inc'd in total.
Rnd 2 Work in seed st, working
increased sts into pat.
Repeat last 2 rnds 3 times more, working
the last rnd with 2 strands of yarn held
tog—11 sts on each needle; 44 sts
in total.
Bind off all sts with 2 strands held tog.

SHOE
With WS facing and beige, begin at first
bound-off st, pick up and k 1 st in each st
under the bound-off edge, picking up 11
sts onto each needle—44 sts total. Join
and place marker for beg of rnd (back of
shoe).
Rnds 1–4 Knit.

SHAPE TOP
Continue in St st (knit wvrnd)
as follows:
Rnd 5 K9, p1, k24, p1, k9.
Rnd 6 K9, p1, k1, [k2tog, k2] 5 times,
k2tog, k1, p1, k9—38 sts.
Rnd 7 K9, p1, k18, p1, k9.
Rnd 8 K9, p1, [k2tog, k2] 4 times,
k2tog, p1, k9—33 sts.
Rnd 9 K9, p1, k13, p1, k9.
Rnd 10 K9, p1, [k2tog] 3 times, k1,
[k2tog] 3 times, p1, k9—27 sts.
Knit 12 rnds.

Bind off loosely as follows:
*K2tog, return st to LH needle; rep
from * until all sts are bound off.

FINISHING
Sew sole seam. Weave in ends.

Repeat from beginning for second shoe. ●

SIZE
6-9 MONTHS

Fringed Boots

There's more than a hint of the Wild West about these fun fringed boot, embellished with side zips.

MATERIALS

1 3½oz/100g ball (220yd/200m) of Cascade 220 Superwash (wool) in beige
1 3½oz/100g hank (150yd/137.5m) of Cascade 220 Superwash Aran (wool) in taupe
1 set (5) size 7 (4.5mm) dpn
Crochet hook size G-6 (4mm)
4 zippers 2½"/6cm
Sewing needle & thread
Stitch marker
Yarn needle

GAUGE

19 sts and 36 rows to 4"/10cm over garter st using size 7 (4.5mm) needles and 220 Superwash Aran.
TAKE TIME TO CHECK GAUGE.

SOLE

With taupe, cast on 32 sts. Divide sts evenly over 4 needles (8 sts per needle). Join, taking care not to twist sts, and place marker for beg of rnd (back of shoe).
Work in garter st in rnds (purl 1 rnd, knit 1 rnd) as follows:
Rnd 1 Purl.
Rnd 2 Needle 1: K1, M1, knit to end; Needle 2: Knit to last st, M1, k1; Needle 3: K1, M1, knit to end; Needle 4: Knit to last st, M1, k1—1 st inc'd on each needle; 4 sts inc'd in total.

Repeat last 2 rnds 5 times more—14 sts per needle; 56 sts in total.
Purl 2 rnds. Cut taupe.

SHOE

Join beige and work as follows:
Next rnd K20, [M1, k2] 8 times, k20—64 sts.

BACK PIECE

Next row (RS) K12, slip rem 2 sts on Needle 1 to Needle 2, turn.
Next row (WS) P24, sl rem 2 sts on Needle 4 to Needle 3, turn.
Continue over 24 sts on Needles 4 and 1 only in stockinette st in rows (knit on RS, purl on WS) for 25 rows more.
Knit next row on WS for turning ridge.
Knit 1 row, purl 1 row.
Bind off all sts of back piece.

FRONT PIECE

With RS facing, join beige to Needle 2 and work in rows over rem 40 sts as follows:
Next row (RS) K6, [k2tog, k3] 5 times, k2tog, k7—34 sts.
Purl 1 row, knit 1 row, purl 1 row.
Next row (RS) K2, [k2tog, k2] 7 times, k2tog, k2—26 sts.
Purl 1 row, knit 1 row, purl 1 row.
Next row (RS) K6, [k2tog] 7 times, k6—19 sts.
Cont in St st in rows for 16 rows more.

Knit next row on WS for turning ridge.
Knit 1 row, purl 1 row.
Bind off all sts of front piece.

HEEL

With taupe, cast on 8 sts. Divide sts evenly over 4 needles (2 sts per needle). Join, taking care not to twist sts, and place marker for beg of rnd.
Work in garter st in rnds as follows:
Rnd 1 Purl.
Rnd 2 Needle 1: K1, M1, knit to end; Needle 2: Knit to last st, M1, k1; Needle 3: K1, M1, knit to end; Needle 4: Knit to last st, M1, k1—1 st inc'd on each needle; 4 sts inc'd in total.
Repeat last 2 rnds 4 times more—28 sts.
Bind off.

FINISHING

Sew sole seam.

Fold hems of front and back pieces to WS at turning ridge and sew in place.
Sew heel seam and sew to the back sole.

FRONT DECORATION

With beige, cast on 24 sts. Purl 1 row.
Bind off as follows:
*K2tog, return st to LH needle; rep
from * until all sts are bound off.

BACK DECORATION

With beige, cast on 26 sts and work in
the same manner as front decoration.
Cut 16 lengths of yarn, each 4"/10cm long.
Add fringe as follows:
Fold 1 length of yarn in half, use crochet
hook to pull loop through back decoration,
pull legs of yarn through loop, tighten to
secure in place.
Rep for rem lengths of yarn, attaching
evenly around.

Sew front and back decorations in place
around ankle of boot (see photo).

Sew in zippers on each side of boot,
making sure zipper slides smoothly.

Weave in ends.

Repeat from beginning for second shoe. ●

Snow Boots

Time to hit the slopes, make a snowman, or maybe just cuddle up with some hot chocolate. Whichever activity you choose, keep those toes toasty in lace-up snow boots

MATERIALS

1 3½oz/100g ball (220yd/200m) of Cascade 220 Superwash (wool) each in blue, dark blue, and white
1 3½oz/100g hank (150yd/137.5m) of Cascade 220 Superwash Aran (wool) in gray
1 set (5) size 5 and 7 (3.75 and 4.5mm) dpn
Crochet hook size E-4 (3.5mm)
12 metal eyelets
Stitch marker
Yarn needle

GAUGE

19 sts and 36 rows to 4"/10cm over garter st using larger needles and 220 Superwash Aran.
TAKE TIME TO CHECK GAUGE.

SOLE

With larger needles and gray, cast on 24 sts. Divide sts evenly over 4 needles (6 sts per needle). Join, taking care not to twist sts, and place marker for beg of rnd (back of shoe).
Work in garter st in rnds (purl 1 rnd, knit 1 rnd) as follows:
Rnd 1 Purl.
Rnd 2 Needle 1: K1, M1, knit to end;
Needle 2: Knit to last st, M1, k1;
Needle 3: K1, M1, knit to end;
Needle 4: Knit to last st, M1, k1—1 st inc'd on each needle; 4 sts inc'd in total.
Repeat last 2 rnds 3 times more—10 sts per needle; 40 sts in total.
Cut gray.

SHOE

Change to smaller needles.
Join blue and work as follows:
Inc rnd Needle 1: [K1, M1] twice, knit to end;
Needle 2: Knit to last 2 sts, [M1, k1] twice;
Needle 3: [K1, M1] twice, knit to end;
Needle 4: Knit to last 2 sts, [M1, k1] twice—12 sts per needle; 48 sts in total.
Purl 1 round, knit 5 rounds
Cut blue. Join dark blue.
Next rnd *K1, sl 1 st wyif; rep from * around.
Knit 3 rounds.

BEGIN SHORT ROWS

Next rnd K21, k2tog, k2, k2tog, k6, turn, work double st (see page 62);
P15, turn, work double st;
K2, k2tog, k2, k2tog, k2, k2tog, k1, turn, work double st;
P8, turn, work double st;
K1, [k2tog] twice, k1, turn, work double st;
P2, turn, work double st;
Knit all sts to end of rnd, working double sts tog with corresponding sts on needle.
Next rnd Knit, working rem double sts tog with corresponding sts on needle and k2tog over 2 center front sts—40 sts.
Knit 2 rounds.
Next rnd K17, k2tog, k2, k2tog, k17—38 sts.
Continue in stripes as follows:
Knit 8 rounds with dark blue.
Knit 2 rounds with white.
Knit 5 rounds with dark blue.
Knit 2 rounds with white. Cut white.
Work with dark blue to end as follows:
Knit 6 rounds.
Next rnd K16, k2tog, yo, k1, yo, k2tog, k17.
Knit next round, working k1 into each yo.
Purl 1 round for turning ridge.
Knit 3 rounds for hem. Bind off all sts.

FINISHING

Sew sole seam.
Fold hem to WS at turning ridge and sew in place.

HEEL CAP

With smaller needles and blue, cast on 16 sts. Work stockinette st in rows (knit on RS, purl on WS) for 4 rows, then dec 1 st each side every other row 5 times.
Bind off all sts. Sew cap to back of heel.

Weave in ends.

Sew on the metal eyelets (see photos).
With crochet hook and blue, make one chain 35"/90cm long and one chain 14½"/37cm long.
Thread the longer chain through the metal eyelets, wrap around shoe once, then tie in a bow.
Thread the shorter chain through the hem, using a safety pin to help, if needed.

With white and yarn needle, embroider the cuff (see photos).

Repeat from beginning for second shoe. ●

Farmer Boots

These sturdy wool boots will have little ones ready to
tackle whatever weather the day brings.

MATERIALS
1 3½oz/100g ball (220yd/200m)
of Cascade 220 Superwash (wool)
in olive
1 3½oz/100g hank (150yd/137.5m)
of Cascade 220 Superwash Aran (wool)
in beige
1 set (5) each size 5 and 7
(3.75 and 4.5mm) dpn
2 beige zippers 2–2½"/5–6 cm long
Stitch marker
Yarn needle

GAUGE
19 sts and 36 rows to 4"/10cm over
garter st using larger needles and 220
Superwash Aran.
TAKE TIME TO CHECK GAUGE.

SOLE
With larger needles and beige, cast on 32
sts. Divide sts evenly over 4 needles (8
sts per needle). Join, taking care not to
twist sts, and place marker for beg of rnd
(back of shoe).
Work in garter st in rnds (purl 1 rnd,
knit 1 rnd) as follows:
Rnd 1 Purl.
Rnd 2 Needle 1: K1, M1, knit to end;
Needle 2: Knit to last st, M1, k1;
Needle 3: K1, M1, knit to end;

Needle 4: Knit to last st, M1, k1—1 st
inc'd on each needle; 4 sts inc'd in total.
Repeat last 2 rnds 3 times more—12 sts
per needle; 48 sts in total.
Purl 1 round, knit 4 rounds. Cut beige.

SHOE
Join olive. Knit 2 rounds.

BEGIN SHORT ROWS
Note When working over a double st,
always work tog with corresponding st
on needle.
Next rnd K27, turn, work double st (see
page 62);
P5, turn, work double st;
K7, turn, work double st;
P10, turn, work double st;
K12, turn, work double st;
P14, turn, work double st;
K16, turn, work double st;
P17, turn, work double st, k to end of rnd.
Knit 1 round.
Next rnd K16, [k2tog] 8 times, k16—40
sts.
Next rnd Knit.
Next rnd K16, [k2tog] 4 times, k16—36
sts.
Next rnd Knit.
Next rnd K16, [k2tog] twice, k16—34
sts.
Next rnd K16, k2tog, k16—33 sts.

Divide the boot leg in half as follows:
Next row (RS) K16, bind off center st,
turn.
Continue to work over all sts in St st in
rows (knit on RS, purl on WS) for 12
rows more.
Knit next row on WS for turing ridge.
Knit 1 row, then purl 1 row for hem.
Bind off all sts.

FINISHING
Sew sole seam.
Sew in zipper to center front opening.
Fold hem to WS at turning ridge and sew
in place.
Weave in ends.

BACK HEEL STRAP
With smaller needles and olive, cast on 6
sts. Divide sts over 2 needles and join to
work in rounds.
Knit 22 rounds. Bind off all sts.
Fold strap in half lengthwise and sew
loop to center back of top of boot.

Repeat from beginning for second shoe. ●

33

Eye-Catchers

Sporty, trendy, cute-as-a-button:

for days when ordinary kicks just won't do the trick.

Basketball Shoes

Just because you don't have the height yet
doesn't mean the gear can't make you look like a star.

MATERIALS

1 3½oz/100g ball
(220yd/200m) of Cascade 220
Superwash (wool) each in white,
red, navy, and royal blue
1 set (5) size 5 (3.75mm) dpn
Crochet hook size E-4 (3.5mm)
Stitch marker
Yarn needle

GAUGE

22 sts and 44 rows to 4"/10cm over
garter st using size 5 (3.75mm) needles.
TAKE TIME TO CHECK GAUGE.

SOLE

With white, cast on 32 sts. Divide sts
evenly over 4 needles (8 sts per needle).
Join, taking care not to twist sts, and
place marker for beg of rnd (back of
shoe).
Work in garter st in rnds (purl 1 rnd,
knit 1 rnd) as follows:
Rnd 1 Purl.
Rnd 2 Needle 1: K1, M1, knit to end;

Needle 2: Knit to last st, M1, k1;
Needle 3: K1, M1, knit to end;
Needle 4: Knit to last st, M1, k1—1 st
inc'd on each needle; 4 sts inc'd in total.
Repeat last 2 rnds 3 times more—12 sts
per needle; 48 sts in total.
With white, purl 4 rounds, knit 1 round.
Cut white.

SHOE

Join navy. Purl 1 round. Cut navy.

TOE

Sl first 5 sts on Needle 2 to Needle 1; sl
first 7 sts on Needle 3 to Needle 2; sl rem
5 sts on Needle 3 to Needle 4—17 sts each
on Needles 1 and 4, 14 sts on Needle 2.
Keeping sts of Needles 1 and 4 on hold,
join red from RS and work in rows on
Needle 2 as follows:
Rows 1–4 Work in St st in rows (knit
on RS, purl on WS).
Row 5 K2, k2tog, k6, k2tog, k2—12 sts.
Rows 6, 8, and 10 Purl.
Row 7 K2, k2tog, k4, k2tog, k2—10 sts.
Row 9 Knit.

Row 11 K2, k2tog, k2, k2tog, k2—8 sts.
Row 12 Purl.
Bind off all sts.

SIDES AND BACK

Set-up row 1 (RS) With RS facing and
first ball of royal blue, pick up and k 1 st
in each of last 2 red sts of toe, then k2 sts
from Needle 4; with navy, k30 sts from
Needles 4 and 1; with 2nd ball of royal
blue, k last 2 sts on Needle 1, then pick up
and k 1 st in each of first 2 sts of toe—38
sts.
Note Do not carry unused yarns. When
changing colors, twist yarns on WS to
prevent holes in work.
Row 2 (WS) With royal blue, k4; with
navy, purl to last 4 sts; with royal blue,
k4.
Continue to work first and last 4 sts in
garter st (knit every row) with royal blue
and center sts in stockinette stitch with
navy, as follows:
Dec row 3 (RS) With royal blue, k4;
with navy, k2tog, k to last 2 navy sts,
k2tog; with royal blue, k4.

Row 4 Work even in pats.
Dec/eyelet row 5 With royal blue, k2,
yo, k2tog (eyelet); with navy, K2tog, k
to last 2 navy sts, k2tog; with royal blue,
k2tog, yo, k2 (eyelet).
Row 6 Repeat row 4.
Repeat rows 3–6 for 3 times more.
Cut navy. With 1 ball of royal blue, knit 4
rows over all sts.
Bind off as follows:
*K2tog, return st to LH needle; rep
from * until all sts are bound off.

FINISHING
Sew sole seams. Weave in ends.

SHOELACE
With crochet hook and white, chain 100.
Fasten off.
Thread shoelace through eyelet holes.

Repeat from beginning for second shoe. ●

Canvas Shoes

The days are long and meant for running around,
and these shoes are comfy enough to run around in all day.

MATERIALS

1 3½oz/100g ball
(220yd/200m) of Cascade 220
Superwash (wool) each
in light pink and white
1 set (5) size 6 (4mm) dpn
Crochet hook size E/4 (3.5mm)
Stitch marker
Yarn needle

GAUGE

22 sts and 44 rows to 4"/10cm over
garter st using size 6 (4mm) needles.
TAKE TIME TO CHECK GAUGE.

SOLE

With white, cast on 32 sts. Divide sts
evenly over 4 needles (8 sts per needle).
Join, taking care not to twist sts, and
place marker for beg of rnd (back of
shoe).
Work in garter st in rnds (purl 1 rnd,
knit 1 rnd) as follows:
Rnd 1 Purl.
Rnd 2 Needle 1: K1, M1, knit to end;
Needle 2: Knit to last st, M1, k1;
Needle 3: K1, M1, knit to end;
Needle 4: Knit to last st, M1, k1—1 st
inc'd on each needle; 4 sts inc'd in total.

Repeat last 2 rnds 5 times more—14 sts
per needle; 56 sts in total.
Cut white.

TONGUE

Slip first 6 sts of Needle 2 to Needle 1;
slip first 8 sts of Needle 3 to Needle 2;
slip rem 6 sts of Needle 3 to Needle
4—20 sts each on Needles 1 and 4,
16 sts on Needle 2.
Keeping sts of Needles 1 and 4 on hold,
join pink and work back and forth in
rows on Needle 2 as follows:
Row 1 (RS) Knit.
Row 2 [K1, p2] 5 times, k1.
Row 3 Knit.
Row 4 Rep row 2.
Row 5 K4, [k2tog, k1] twice, k2tog,
k4—13 sts.
Row 6 K1, p2, [k1, p1] 3 times, k1, p2,
k1.
Row 7 Knit.
Row 8 Rep row 6.
Row 9 Knit.
Row 10 Rep row 6.
Row 11 K1, k2tog, k to last 3 sts, k2tog,
k1—11 sts.
Row 12 *K1, p1; rep from * to last st,
k1.
Row 13 Knit.

Rows 14–21 Rep rows 12 and 13 four
times more.
Row 22 K2tog, [p1, k1], 3 times, p1,
k2tog—9 sts.
Row 23 K2tog, k5, k2tog—7 sts.
Bind off all sts.

SIDES AND BACK

With pink, work the sts of Needles 1 and
4 back and forth in rows as follows:
Row 1 (RS) At beg of Needle 4, cast on 6
sts, then beg with the 6 cast-on sts, work
as follows: k2, M1, [k5, M1] 7 times, k3,
cast on 6 sts at end of Needle 1—60 sts.
Row 2 (WS) K2, [p1, k1] twice, p to last
6 sts, [k1, p1] twice, k2.
Rows 3 and 4 K the knit sts and p the purl
sts.
Eyelet row 5 K1, p1, k1, yo, k2tog, p1,
k2tog, k to last 8 sts, k2tog, p1, k2tog,
yo, k1, p1, k1—58 sts.
Row 6 K the knit sts and p the purl sts,
working each yo as a purl st.
Row 7 [K1, p1] 3 times, k2tog, k to last
8 sts, k2tog, [p1, k1] 3 times—56 sts.
Row 8 K the knit sts and p the purl sts.
Repeat rows 5–8 for 3 times more.
Repeat row 6 once more. Bind off all sts.

FINISHING
Sew sole seam.

HEEL PATCH
With pink, cast on 9 sts.
Rows 1 and 3 (RS) [K1, p1] 4 times, k1.
Rows 2 and 4 Knit.
Row 5 K2tog, [k1, p1] twice, k1, k2tog.
Row 6 Knit.
Row 7 K2tog, k1, p1, k1, k2tog.
Row 8 Knit.
Bind off all sts.
Sew on the heel patch at the back of
the shoe.

Weave in ends.

SHOELACE
With crochet hook and pink, chain 120.
Fasten off.
Thread shoelaces through eyelet holes.
Stitch ends of the shoelaces to neaten.

Repeat from beginning for second shoe. ●

SIZE
3-6 MONTHS

Sneakers

This nifty pair hearkens back to
the colorful sneakers heyday of the '80s.

MATERIALS

1 3½oz/100g ball (246yd/225m)
of Cascade Sunseeker
(cotton/acrylic) each
in white and gray
1 3½oz/100g ball (220yd/200m)
of Cascade Northshore (acrylic)
in blue and light blue with metallic
Small amount of silver lurex
embroidery thread
Small amount of a chunky yarn
in white (for shoelaces)
1 set (5) each size 3 and 5
(3.25 and 3.75mm) dpn
1 spare size 5 (3.75mm) dpn
Sewing needle
Stitch markers
Large yarn needle

GAUGE

22 sts and 44 rows to 4"/10cm over
garter st using larger needles.
TAKE TIME TO CHECK GAUGE.

SOLE

With white and larger needles, cast on
32 sts. Divide sts evenly over 4 needles
(8 sts per needle). Join, taking care not
to twist sts, and place marker for beg of
rnd (back of shoe).
Work in garter st in rnds (purl 1 rnd,
knit 1 rnd) as follows:
Rnd 1 Purl.

Rnd 2 Needle 1: K1, M1, knit to end;
Needle 2: Knit to last st, M1, k1;
Needle 3: K1, M1, knit to end;
Needle 4: Knit to last st, M1, k1—1 st
inc'd on each needle; 4 sts inc'd in total.
Repeat last 2 rnds 5 times more—14 sts
per needle; 56 sts in total.
Purl 2 rnds.

BEGIN SHORT ROWS

Work wedge as foll:
Rnd 1 *P14, turn, work double st (see
page 62);
K28, turn, work double st;
P14. You have returned to beg of rnd.*
Knit next rnd over all sts, working double
sts tog with corresponding sts on needle.
Mark this round.
Purl 2 rnds.
Repeat from * to * once more.
Knit next rnd over all sts (turning ridge),
working double sts tog with correspond-
ing sts on needle.
Purl 2 rnds.
Fold piece so knit side shows on RS.
***With spare needle, pick up and k 14
sts along marked rnd in line with sts on
Needle 1. Hold the spare needle with the
picked up sts parallel to the sts on Nee-
dle 1.
Insert 3rd needle knitwise into first st
on both needles and k them tog. **Insert
3rd needle into next st on both needles
and k them tog, pass the first st over the
2nd st on 3rd needle to bind off; rep

from ** until all sts on spare needle and
Needle 1 have been bound off.
Repeat from *** for Needles 2, 3, and 4
so that all sts are bound off.
Pick up and k sts along top of bound-off
edge as follows:
14 sts each on Needles 1 and 4, 15 sts
each on Needles 2 and 3—58 sts.
Knit 6 rnds.
Rnd 7 K18, [k2tog, k2] 5 times, k2tog,
k18—52 sts.
Rnd 8 K14, work k1, p1 rib over next
24 sts, k14.
Rnd 9 K16, k2tog, k1, [k2tog] 7 times,
k1, k2tog, k16—43 sts.
Rnd 10 K13, work k1, p1 rib over 17 sts,
k13.
Rnd 11 K16, p2tog, k1, p2tog, k2tog,
p2tog, k2tog, k16—38 sts.
Rnd 12 K17, bind off 4 sts, k to end—
34 sts.
Continue to work back and forth in rows
as follows:
Row 1 K17 to end of Needle 1.
Row 2 Bind off 7 sts, p to end of Needle 4.
Row 3 Bind off 7 sts, k to end of Needle 1.
Bind off all sts on WS.

TONGUE

With white and larger needles, cast on 6
sts. Working back and forth in rows,
work in St st (knit on RS, purl on WS)
for 20 rows. Bind off. Sew the tongue in
front of the shoe opening.

BLUE APPLIQUES FOR SOLE (MAKE 2)

With blue and smaller needles, cast on 14 sts.

Row 1 (RS) Purl.

Change to larger needles.

Row 2 Bind off 2 sts, k to end.

Row 3 Purl.

Row 4 Bind off 3 sts, k to end.

Bind off rem 9 sts.

Work a second piece in the same way.

GRAY APPLIQUES FOR SOLE (MAKE 2)

With gray and larger needles, cast on 31 sts.

Row 1 (RS) Purl.

Row 2 K2tog, k to end—30 sts.

Row 3 Bind off 4 sts, p to last 2 sts, p2tog—26 sts.

Row 4 Bind off 12 sts, k to end.

Row 5 Bind off 2 sts, p to end.

Row 6 Bind off 5 sts, k to end.

Row 7 Bind off 1 st, p to end—5 sts.

Row 8 K2tog, k3.

Row 9 P2tog, p2.

Bind off all sts.

Work a second piece, reversing shaping as follows:

Row 1 (RS) Purl.

Row 2 Bind off 4 sts, k to last 2 sts, k2tog—26 sts.

Row 3 P2tog, purl to end—25 sts.

Row 4 Bind off 2 sts, k to end.

Row 5 Bind off 12 sts, p to end.

Row 6 Bind off 1 st, k to end.

Row 7 Bind off 5 st, p to end—5 sts.

Row 8 K3, k2tog.

Row 9 P2, p2tog.

Bind off all sts.

SMALL BLUE FRONT APPLIQUES FOR BOTH SIDES OF THE CLOSURE (MAKE 2)

With blue and smaller needles, cast on 7 sts. Knit 1 row, purl 1 row, knit 1 row. Bind off all sts.

Work a second piece in the same way.

HEART APPLIQUES (MAKE 2)

With blue and smaller needles, cast on 7 sts.

Purl 1 row on RS, then work 4 rows in rev St st (p on RS, k on WS).

Next row (WS) K2tog, k3, k2tog.

Next row Purl.

Next row K2tog, k1, k2tog

Next row K3tog.

Fasten off last st

Work a second piece in the same way.

BACK CENTER PIECE

With light blue metallic and smaller needles, cast on 7 sts.

Row 1 (RS) Purl.

Row 2 K1, M1, k5, M1, k1—9 sts.

Row 3 Purl.

Row 4 K1, M1, k7, M1, k1—11 sts.

Row 5 Purl.

Row 6 K1, M1, k9, M1, k1—13 sts.

Row 7 Cast on 12 sts, k to end.

Row 8 Cast on 12 sts, p to end—37 sts.

Rows 9–12 Work in St st.

Row 13 Bind off 12 sts, k to end.

Row 14 Bind off 12 sts, p to end.

Row 15 K2tog, k9, k2tog—11 sts.

Row 16 Purl.

Row 17 K2tog, k7, k2tog—9 sts.

Bind off all sts.

CENTER FRONT SOLE APPLIQUE

With blue and smaller needles, cast on 16 sts.

Purl 1 row. Knit 1 row.

Next row Bind off 5 sts, p to end.

Next row Bind off 5 sts, k to end.

Bind off all sts.

FINISHING

Sew sole seam. Sew on all appliques (see photos).

If desired, embroider small icon with silver lurex embroidery yarn on outside edge. If desired, embroider lettering with the thin white yarn on the side heel. Weave in ends.

For the shoelaces, cut 1 length of chunky white wool yarn approx 23½"/60cm long. Thread shoelaces on front piece and make a knot on each end of the lace.

Repeat from beginning for second shoe. ●

SIZE
6-9 MONTHS

Loafers

Stylish, go-with-everything slip-ons are equally at home ambling around the house or dressing up to go out.

MATERIALS

1 3½oz/100g ball (220yd/200m) of Cascade 220 Superwash (wool) each in light blue and white
1 1¾oz/50g ball (135yd/124m) of DMC Woolly (merino wool) in brown
1 set (5) size 5 (3.75mm) dpn
Stitch marker
Yarn needle

GAUGE

22 sts and 44 rows to 4"/10cm over garter st using size 5 (3.75mm) needles and 220 Superwash.
TAKE TIME TO CHECK GAUGE.

PATTERN STITCH (IN ROUNDS)

Rnds 1 and 2 Knit.
Rnds 3 and 4 *K2, p2; rep from * to end.
Rnds 5 and 6 Knit.
Rnds 7 and 8 *P2, k2; rep from * to end.
Repeat rnds 1–8 for pattern st in rounds.

PATTERN STITCH (IN ROWS)

Row 1 (RS) Knit.
Row 2 Purl.
Row 3 *K2, p2; rep from * to end.
Row 4 Knit the k sts and p the purl sts.
Row 5 Knit.
Row 6 Purl.
Row 7 *P2, k2; rep from * to end.
Row 8 Knit the k sts and p the purl sts.
Repeat rows 1–8 for pattern st in rows.

SOLE

With white, cast on 40 sts.
Divide sts evenly over 4 needles (10 sts per needle). Join, taking care not to twist sts, and place marker for beg of rnd (back of shoe).
Work in garter st in rnds (purl 1 rnd, knit 1 rnd) as follows:
Rnd 1 Purl.
Rnd 2 Needle 1: K1, M1, knit to end; Needle 2: Knit to last st, M1, k1; Needle 3: K1, M1, knit to end; Needle 4: Knit to last st, M1, k1—1 st inc'd on each needle; 4 sts inc'd in total.
Repeat last 2 rnds 5 times more—16 sts per needle; 64 sts in total.
Purl 2 rnds. Cut white.

HEEL

Work on Needles 4 and 1 only as follows:
With RS facing, join light blue to beg of Needle 4.
Rows 1 and 2 Knit.
Repeat rows 1 and 2 with white.
Cut white and light blue.

SHOE

Cont to work in rnds over all needles as follows:
With RS facing, join brown at beg of rnd (Needle 1).
Knit 1 rnd, purl 1 rnd. Cut brown.
Join light blue and work in pattern stitch in rounds for 4 rounds.

Rnd 5 K20, [k2tog] 12 times, k20—52 sts.
Rnd 6 K14, [k2tog, k1] 8 times, k14—44 sts.
Work rnds 7 and 8 of pattern st once, then rnds 1–6 once more.

FRONT RISE

With a separate length of blue yarn, bind off center back 22 sts (11 sts at end of rnd and 11 sts at beg of rnd).
Starting with row 7 of pattern st in rows, work the remaining 22 sts in pattern as follows:
Next row K2tog, work in pattern to last 2 sts, k2tog.
Repeat last row 3 times more.
Bind off all sts.

FINISHING

Sew sole seam.

SIDE DETAIL (MAKE 2)

With brown, cast on 6 sts and work in stockinette st in rows (knit 1 row, purl 1 row) for 13 rows. Bind off.
Make a second piece in the same way.
Sew to shoe, angled, to each side of shoe just before front rise.
Weave in ends.

Repeat from beginning for second shoe. ●

Summer, Sun, Sandals

Light, breathable shoes and sandals let the sunshine in.

SIZE
0-3 MONTHS

Strappy Sandals

On hot summer days, these strappy, sporty sandals
are the next best things to bare feet.

MATERIALS

1 3½oz/100g ball (220yd/200m)
of Cascade 220 Superwash (wool)
each in red, steel blue, and white
1 set (5) size 5 (3.75mm) dpn
1 spare size 5 (3.75mm) dpn
2 small buttons, 3/8"/1cm
Stitch marker
Yarn needle

GAUGE

22 sts and 44 rows to 4"/10cm over
garter st using size 5 (3.75mm) needles.
TAKE TIME TO CHECK GAUGE.

SOLE

With steel blue, cast on 32 sts. Divide sts
evenly over 4 needles (8 sts per needle).
Join, taking care not to twist sts and
place marker for beg of rnd (back of
shoe).
Work in garter st in rnds (purl 1 rnd,
knit 1 rnd) as follows:
Rnd 1 Purl.
Rnd 2 Needle 1: K1, M1, knit to end;
Needle 2: Knit to last st, M1, k1;
Needle 3: K1, M1, knit to end;
Needle 4: Knit to last st, M1, k1—1 st
inc'd on each needle; 4 sts inc'd in total.
Repeat last 2 rnds 3 times more—12 sts
per needle; 48 sts in total.

Knit 1 round, purl 1 round (mark this
rnd), then purl 3 rounds more.
Fold the last few rounds so that the knit
side is to the RS.
*With spare needle, pick up and k 12 sts
along marked rnd in line with sts on
Needle 1. Hold the spare needle with
the picked up sts parallel to the sts on
Needle 1.
Insert 3rd needle knitwise into first st
on both needles and k them tog. **Insert 3rd needle into next st on both needles and k them tog, pass the 1st st over
the 2nd st on 3rd needle to bind off; rep
from ** until all sts on spare needle and
Needle 1 have been bound off.
Repeat from * for Needles 2, 3, and 4
so that all sts are bound off.

STRAPS (MAKE 3)

With red, cast on 5 sts.
Work I-cord as follows:
Row 1 (RS) K5, do not turn. Slide sts to
right tip of needle, pulling your across
back of work to work next row from RS.
Repeat row 1 for 22 rows. Bind off all sts.

Make a second strap in the same manner.
Make a third strap, but work 30 rows of
I-cord before binding off.

FINISHING

Sew sole seam.

Sew the two shorter straps crosswise
along front. Sew the longer strap as a
heel strap and attach one button to the
outer edge (see photo). Weave in ends.

Cut 2 strands of steel blue and 1 strand
of white, each approx 24"/61cm long.
Make a braid with these 3 strands and
sew around the outer edge of the sole
(see photo).

Repeat from beginning for second shoe. ●

Espadrilles

The footwear of choice for little European beachgoers:
nautical stripes and a sole that mimics
the traditional rope bottoms.

MATERIALS

- 1 3½oz/100g ball (220yd/200m)
  of Cascade 220 Superwash (wool)
  each in dark blue and white
- 1 3½oz/100g hank (150yd/137.5m)
  of Cascade 220 Superwash Aran
  (wool) in beige
- 1 set (5) size 7 (4.5mm) dpn
- 1 pair size 4 (3.5mm) needles
- Stitch marker
- Yarn needle

GAUGE

19 sts and 36 rows to 4"/10cm over
garter st using larger needles and 220
Superwash Aran.
TAKE TIME TO CHECK GAUGE.

STRIPE PATTERN

Work in stockinette st in rows (knit on
RS, purl on WS) in stripes as follows:
*2 rows in white, 2 rows in dark blue;
repeat from * (4 rows) for stripe pat.

SOLE

Cut a 24"/61cm length of beige and place
to side for later use during bind off.
With dpn and beige, cast on 32 sts.
Divide sts evenly over 4 needles (8 sts
per needle). Join, taking care not to twist
sts, and place marker for beg of rnd (back
of shoe).
Work in garter st in rnds (purl 1 rnd,
knit 1 rnd) as follows:
Rnd 1 Purl.
Rnd 2 Needle 1: K1, M1, knit to end;

Needle 2: Knit to last st, M1, k1;
Needle 3: K1, M1, knit to end;
Needle 4: Knit to last st, M1, k1—1 st
inc'd on each needle; 4 sts inc'd in total.
Repeat last 2 rnds 3 times more—12 sts
per needle; 48 sts in total.
Bind off with 2 strands of beige held tog
to make the edge more pronounced and
stable.

BACK HEEL PIECE

With straight needles and dark blue, cast
on 10 sts.
Row 1 (WS) K2, p7, k1.
Row 2 (RS) P2, k7, p1.
Repeat rows 1 and 2 until there are 42
rows in total.
Bind off all sts on WS.

STRIPED FRONT PIECE

With sstraight needles and white, cast on
20 sts and work in stripe pat for 9 rows.
Dec row (WS) With white, p2tog, p to
last 2 sts, p2tog—2 sts dec'd.
With dark blue, knit 1 row, purl 1 row.
Cont in stripe pat, dec 1 st each side of
row on next row then every following
row 6 times more—4 sts.
Bind off all sts with white.

FINISHING

Sew sole seam.
Sew the front piece to the front of the
shoe so that the sole is visible from
the outside.

Sew the back heel piece lengthwise along
the back half of the shoe, letting the top
half roll to the WS approx ¼"/.5cm, then
sew the short sides of the back along the
top piece (see photo).

With dark blue, embroider buttonhole st
(see below) along top of the bound-off
sole edge.

Weave in ends.

Repeat from beginning
for second shoe. ●

Moccasins

Keep away the morning dew or evening chill
with comfy cozy moccasins, and do it with fringe-y flair.

MATERIALS

1 3½oz/100g ball (220yd/200m) of
Cascade 220 Superwash (wool) in beige
1 1¾oz/50g ball (135yd/124m)
of DMC Woolly (merino wool) each
in dark brown
1 set (5) size 5 (3.75mm) dpn
Crochet hook size E/4 (3.5mm)
Stitch marker
Yarn needle

GAUGE

23 sts and 28 rows to 4"/10cm over
stockinette st using size 5 (3.75mm)
needles and 220 Superwash.
TAKE TIME TO CHECK GAUGE.

SOLE

With beige, cast on 32 sts. Divide sts
evenly over 4 needles (8 sts per needle).
Join, taking care not to twist sts, and
place marker for beg of rnd (back of
shoe).
Work in stockinette st in rnds (knit every
rnd) as follows:
Rnd 1 Knit.
Rnd 2 Needle 1: K1, M1, knit to end;
Needle 2: Knit to last st, M1, k1;
Needle 3: K1, M1, knit to end;
Needle 4: Knit to last st, M1, k1—1 st
inc'd on each needle; 4 sts inc'd in total.
Repeat last 2 rnds 4 times more—13 sts
per needle; 52 sts in total.

SHOE

Purl 1 round, knit 1 round.
Repeat rnd 2 of sole once more—14 sts
each needle; 56 sts in total.
Knit 4 rounds.
Next rnd K19, bind off 18 sts, k to end of
rnd.
Slip rem sts on Needle 2 to Needle 1.
Slip rem sts on Needle 3 to Needle 4.

BACK

Continue to work back and forth in rows
over 2 needles as follows:
Next row (RS) K19 to end of Needle 1.
Next row Bind off 3 sts, p35 to end of
Needle 4.
Next row Bind off 3 sts, k28, turn, work
double st (see page 62);
P23, turn, work double st;
K20, turn, work double st:
P16, turn, work double st;
K13, turn.
Working double sts tog with correspond-
ing sts on needle, k to end of row on WS.
Cont to work in reverse stockinette st in
rows (purl on RS, knit on WS) over all
sts for 3 rows more.

Bind off as follows:
*K2tog, return st to LH needle; rep
from * until all sts are bound off.
Fold back rise down to outside of shoe
and secure in place. Weave a length of
yarn through back of shoe along center
of folded piece (see photo).

FRONT

With beige, cast on 6 sts and work in
stockinette st in rows (knit on RS, purl on
WS), inc 1 st each side every 2nd row
5 times—16 sts.
Work even until 18 rows have been
worked from beginning.
Cont in reverse stockinette st for 4 rows.
Bind off all sts.

Fit curve of front into the curved front
rise of shoe with knit side showing. With
crochet hook, attach front in place, leav-
ing final 4 rows of reverse stockinette st
unattached.
Fold rem unattached rows to the outside
of front of shoe and secure in place.
Cut 7 lengths of yarn, each 4"/10cm long.
Add fringe as follows:
Fold 1 length of yarn in half, use crochet
hook to pull loop through edge of front
fold, pull legs of yarn through loop, tight-
en to secure in place.
Rep for rem lengths of yarn, attaching
evenly across (see photo).
Trim fringe to approx ½"/1.5cm.

SOLE 2

With dark brown, cast on 16 sts. Divide sts evenly over 4 needles (4 sts per needle). Join, taking care not to twist sts, and place marker for beg of rnd.

Work in garter st in rnds (purl 1 rnd, knit 1 rnd) as follows:

Rnd 1 Purl.

Rnd 2 Needle 1: K1, M1, knit to end; Needle 2: Knit to last st, M1, k1; Needle 3: K1, M1, knit to end; Needle 4: Knit to last st, M1, k1—1 st inc'd on each needle; 4 sts inc'd in total.

Repeat last 2 rnds 4 times more—9 sts per needle; 36 sts in total.

Bind off all sts.

SOLE 3

Cut a 12"/30.5mm length of dark brown and set aside for later use during bind-off. With dark brown, cast on 16 sts and work in the same way as sole 2 until there are 9 sts per needle; 36 sts in total.

Next rnd Bind off 15 sts, leave 6 sts on hold, join extra length of yarn and bind off last 15 sts.

Cont in garter st in rows (knit every row) over rem 6 sts for 5 rows more.

Bind off all sts.

FINISHING

Sew all sole seams.

Fit sole 3 to the back half of the beige sole and sew in place, sewing flap up back of shoe (see photo). Fit sole 2 to the front half of the beige sole and sew in place.

Weave in ends.

Repeat from beginning for second shoe. ●

Slippers

Sometimes there's no need to mess with a classic:
a simple slip-on shoe is practical, snug, and charming.

MATERIALS

1 3½oz/100g ball (220yd/200m)
of Cascade 220 Superwash (wool)
each in white and steel blue
1 set (5) size 5 (3.75mm) dpn
Stitch marker
Yarn needle
Optional: Elastic thread

GAUGE

22 sts and 44 rows to 4"/10cm over
garter st using size 5 (3.75mm) needles.
TAKE TIME TO CHECK GAUGE.

NOTE

If desired, work bind-off of top of shoe
holding yarn with elastic thread to help
pull in top edge.

SOLE

With white, cast on 32 sts. Divide sts
evenly over 4 needles (8 sts per needle).
Join, taking care not to twist sts, and
place marker for beg of rnd (back of
shoe).
Work in garter st in rnds (purl 1 rnd,
knit 1 rnd) as follows:
Rnd 1 Purl.
Rnd 2 Needle 1: K1, M1, knit to end;
Needle 2: Knit to last st, M1, k1;
Needle 3: K1, M1, knit to end;

Needle 4: Knit to last st, M1, k1—1 st
inc'd on each needle; 4 sts inc'd in total.
Repeat last 2 rnds 3 times more—12 sts
per needle; 48 sts in total.
Purl 4 rounds. Cut white.

SHOE

Join steel blue. Knit 1 round, then purl
7 rounds.

Next rnd P36, turn, work double st (see
page 62);
K24, turn, work double st;
[P2tog] 12 times, stop at end of Needle 3.
Place new beg of rnd marker at begin-
ning of Needle 4. Remove old beg of rnd
marker.
Next rnd Purl, working double sts tog
with corresponding sts on needle.
Next rnd Bind off 23 sts (back of shoe),
[p2tog] 6 times, turn, work double st;
Knit to end.
Bind off all sts.

FINISHING

Sew sole seam. Weave in ends.

Repeat from beginning for second shoe. ●

Helpful Information

Knitting Terms and Abbreviations

approx	approximately	pm	place maker
beg	begin(ning)	psso	pass slipped stitch(es) over
CC	contrasting color	purlwise	as if to purl
ch	chain (crochet loop)w	rem	remain(s)(ing)
cm	centimeter(s)	rep	repeat
cn	cable needle	RH	right-hand
cont	continu(e)(ing)	rnd(s)	round(s)
dc	double crochet	RS	right side(s)
dec	decreas(e)(ing)	S2KP	slip 2 stitches together, knit 1 stitch, pass 2 slipped stitches over knit stitch—2 stitches decreased
dec'd	decreased		
dpn	double-pointed needle(s)	sc	single crochet
foll	follow(s)(ing)	SKP	slip 1 stitch, knit 1 stitch, pass slipped stitch over knit stitch—1 stitch decreased
g	gram(s)		
inc	increas(e)(ing)	SK2P	slip 1 stitch, knit 2 stitches together, pass slipped stitch over knit 2 together—2 stitches decreased
inc'd	increased		
k	knit	sl	slip
knitwise	as if to knit	sl st	slip stitch
k2tog	knit 2 stitches together	sm	slip marker
kfb	knit into front and back of stitch—1 stitch increased	ssk (ssp)	slip next 2 stitches knitwise (purlwise) one at a time; knit (purl) these 2 stitches together—1 stitch decreased
LH	left-hand		
lp(s)	loop(s)	sssk	slip next 3 stitches knitwise, one at a time, knit these 3 stitches together—2 stitches decreased
m	meter(s)		
M1	make 1 knit stitch by inserting tip of left needle from front to back under strand between last stitch and next stitch, knit into back loop—1 stitch increased	st(s)	stitch(es)
		St st	stockinette stitch
		tbl	through back loop(s)
		tog	together
M1-p	make 1 purl stitch by inserting tip of left needle from back to front under strand between last stitch and next stitch, purl into front loop—1 stitch increased	tr	treble crochet
		WS	wrong side(s)
		wyib	with yarn in back
MC	main color	wyif	with yarn in front
mm	millimeter(s)	yd	yard(s)
oz	ounce(s)	yo	yarn over needle
p	purl	*	repeat directions following * as many times as indicated
p2tog	purl 2 stitches together	[ ]	repeat directions inside brackets as many times as indicated
pat(s)	pattern(s)		

DOUBLE STITCH (SHORT ROWS)

A double stitch is used when working short rows to alleviate a hole when turning the work.

With yarn in front of work, slip the first stitch on LH needle purlwise to RH needle. Bring the yarn to back of work over the top of the right needle to make a yarn over, pulling yarn tightly. If the yarn is not pulled tightly, there will be a hole in the work. Continue in the pattern as instructed.

When working across a double stitch, work the double stitch together with the corresponding stitch on the needle continuing in the pattern.

Index

sixth&spring books   104 W 27th St, 3rd Floor, New York, NY 10001
www.sixthandspring.com

Editor   Vice President/Editorial
JACOB SEIFERT   Director
                                    TRISHA MALCOLM
Art Directors
JOE VIOR   Chief Operating Officer
DEBORAH GRISORIO   CAROLINE KILMER

Supervising Patterns Editor   Production Manager
CARLA SCOTT   DAVID JOINNIDES

Illustrator   President
SUSANNE BOCHEM   ART JOINNIDES

                                    Chairman
                                    JAY STEIN

Library of Congress Cataloging-in-Publication Data

Names: Spitz, Helga, author.
Title: Classic kicks for little feet : 16 knitted shoe styles for baby's
   first year / by Helga Spitz.
Other titles: Baby-SchuÃàhchen -Tick-Schuhklassiker fuÃàr kleine
FuÃàsse
   stricken. English
Description: First edition. | New York : Sixth&Spring Books, 2018. |
Includes
   index.
Identifiers: LCCN 2017061352 | ISBN 9781640210264 (hardcover)
Subjects: LCSH: Knitting--Patterns. | Baby booties. | Infants' clothing.
Classification: LCC TT825 .S7131713 2018 | DDC 746.43/2--dc23
LC record available at https://lccn.loc.gov/2017061352

Manufactured in China

1 3 5 7 9 10 8 6 4 2

First English Edition